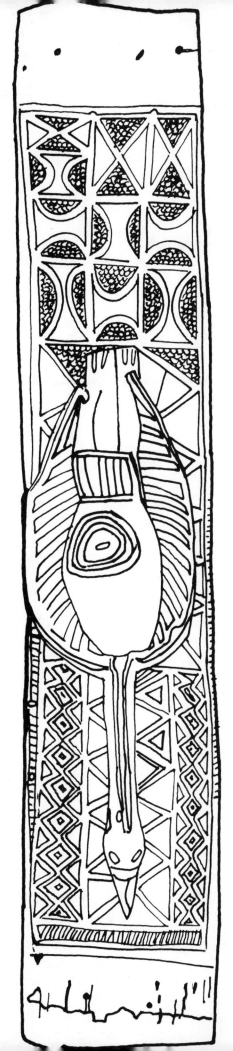

AFRICAN DESIGNS

OF THE CONGO

by Caren Caraway

Stemmer
House
PUBLISHERS, INC.
Owings Mills, Maryland

Inquiries should be directed to
Stemmer House Publishers, Inc.
2627 Caves Road
Owings Mills, Maryland 21117

Printed and bound in the United States of America

A Barbara Holdridge book

First printing 1986
Second printing 1990

Colophon
Designed by Barbara Holdridge
Composed in Times Roman with Aurora Grotesk IX display by
        Brown Composition, Baltimore, Maryland
Color separations by Sun Crown, Washington, D.C.
Printed on 75-pound Williamsburg Offset and bound by Worzalla
        Printers and Binders, Stevens Point, Wisconsin

AFRICAN DESIGNS

OF THE CONGO

Introduction

The great heart of Africa is a vast region of hot, humid rain forest with surrounding areas of parkland and patches of woodland. It is webbed with streams and rivers, among which are the mighty Congo and its tributaries that together embrace an area from the Atlantic Ocean to the lakes of East Africa. There are extreme variations in the environment, but in general the climate has long made cultural development difficult in many areas. Pygmies wander in the dense forest while other peoples cultivate small clearings. Art developed intermittently in these regions.

The open hill country south and east of the Congo provides fertile land for cultivation and hunting, as well as easy access by means of the innumerable rivers for groups of people pressured by other tribes. These people brought with them many influences, including that of sacred kingship from the valley of the Nile.

Great feudal kingdoms were first established when immigrants from the north subjugated the **Bantu.** Most of the people who inhabit this territory speak Bantu languages but are racially mixed and developed different cultures. The people of the northern Congo developed a patriarchal society, while those of the south formed a matriarchal system, although at one time the southern Congo Kingdom was dominated by one in the north.

When the Portuguese discovered the Congo in 1482, they established a relationship with the kingdoms there that lasted for two centuries. It is believed that Hindus arrived in the sixteenth century. Contact with Europeans was established again late in the nineteenth century. Yet there is little evidence of European influence on the variety of early native art which developed as early as the sixteenth century in response to the requirements of the royal courts.

FANG art was created by various **Pangwe** tribes, who made simplified wooden figures and heads for bieri boxes designed to contain either the skull of the founder of a village, the bones of prominent historical figures or slain enemies. The bieri were family protectors considered to be so powerful that they could heal the sick. They were cared for by the head of the family, who did not allow women to see them. White Fang secret society masks were used to drive out wizards and witches.

The **BAKWELE** produced abstract masks, many with heart-shaped faces.

The **BATEKE** lived in the savannah. The carvers belonged to the **Wambundu** tribe. They made highly revered, disc-like masks with symmetrical abstract features of red, black and white.

BAKONGO refers to the style of the lower Congo tribes. For four and a half centuries they were exposed to European influences. The western Bakongo created sculptures with a unified style. Memorial figures of stone and wood were believed to contain the spirits of the dead which gave protection and advice,

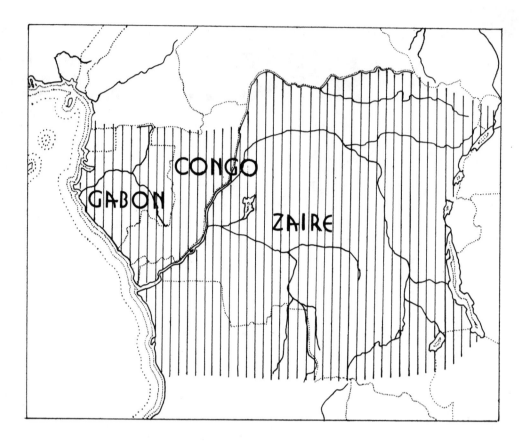

as long as they were honored with sacrifices. Fetishes were charged with magic when the hollowed-out head or body was filled with magical substances and the outlet closed with a mirror. Some were studded with nails to grant wishes or curses, and to summon spirits to seek revenge. Spirits of the dead entered the fetishes to heal the sick, protect hunters and warriors, stimulate love or discover robbers. Masks were used in initiation ceremonies.

In the southwestern Congo the **BAYAKA** were known as great warriors and hunters. Their helmet masks represented supernatural forces and were used to celebrate initiation into the men's society. No wish or gift could be refused when the masks were worn.

The **BAHOLO** produced highly stylized works and the **BASUKU,** related to the Bayaka, created their own style.

The **BAPENDE** were divided by the River Loange into two groups with different styles. The western group carved more naturalistic masks and figures to adorn household objects, while the eastern group produced geometric works related to the Bateke.

The **BUSHONGO** was a powerful state with a divine king and sophisticated court devoted to a peaceful way of life. Both an aristocratic and plebeian style of art were developed, with patterned decoration abundantly applied to all items.

The **BAKUBA** kingdom of tribes, ruled by the Bushongo, flourished in the hill country of the central Congo. It also maintained a sacral kingship, whose light-skinned ancestors migrated from the north fifteen hundred years ago. The arts were encouraged by the court aristocracy and artists were honored. They created memorial statuary but little other non-functional figures. Bakuba masks were decorated with glass beads, feathers, copper, hair, cloth and cowrie shells.

The **BATCHOKWE** were distinguished carvers, hunters and warriors subjected for a time to the mighty Balunda Kingdom. They had sacred kingship and ritual eating of human flesh. The Batchokwe created naturalistic royal statues and several kinds of masks. Some were incarnations of powerful spirits which granted fertility, others symbolized ancestors, and a third kind was used in dances.

The **BENA KANIOKA** were part of the Baluba Kingdom, but preserved their own political independence. Their bold masks, with open mouths and snarling teeth seemed almost aggressive.

The **BASONGE** formed a patriarchal culture in the middle of the matriarchal Bantu society. They developed a different style of sculpture as well, with hard-faceted planes and sharp angular edges. The fetishes were decorated with snakeskin, feathers, shells and beads. The magical power of the masks was maintained with blood sacrifices.

The **BALUBA** deposed the king of the Basonge and formed a powerful military federation of different Bantu tribes, until it was conquered by the Batchokwe and Bayaka in the nineteenth century. They revered women and gave them high status. The image of the female spirit as a deified first mother was represented in naturalistic, swelling, rounded carvings that invoke her power. There were variations in positions and style but they differed in proportions and details.

The **BASIKASINGO (KASIKASINGO)** modified the round style of the Baluba into sterner abstracted forms.

The **ABABUA** developed simplified black and white masks to bring luck in hunting in the jungle and swamps where they lived.

The **BAMBOLE** were farmers and hunters governed by a society that used figures as warnings. Abstract masks were used in initiation rituals.

The **AZENDE** spread over a wide region after migrating from the central Sudan in the sixteenth century. Their sculptures were fairly abstract.

European political and religious influences have contributed to the decline of the art of the Congo. It is doubtful that great works will again be created to serve a religious function in African life. It is even questionable whether the tradition of fine secular art can be maintained.

C.C.

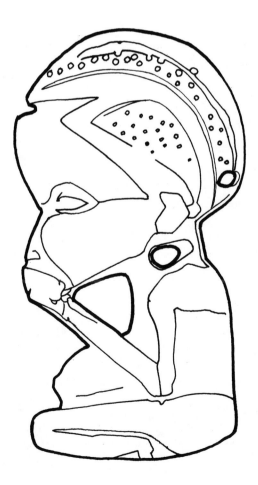

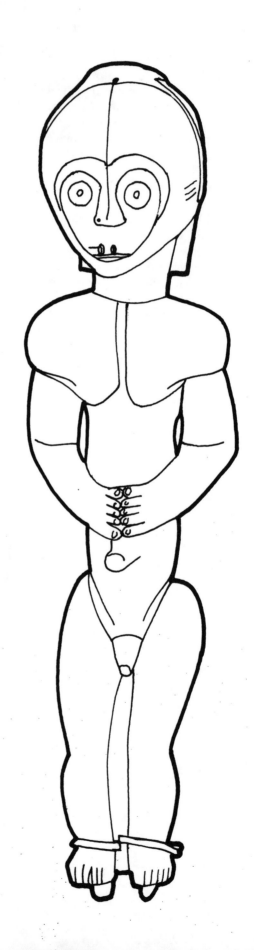

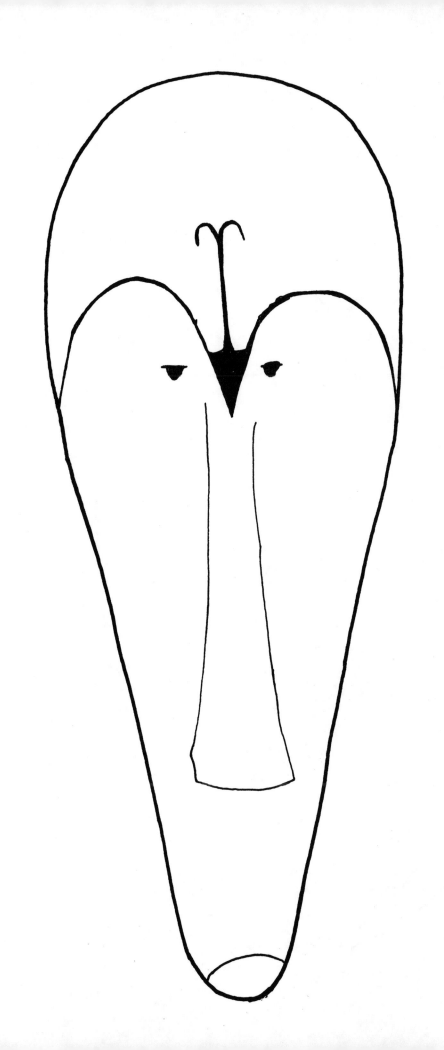

BAKWELE

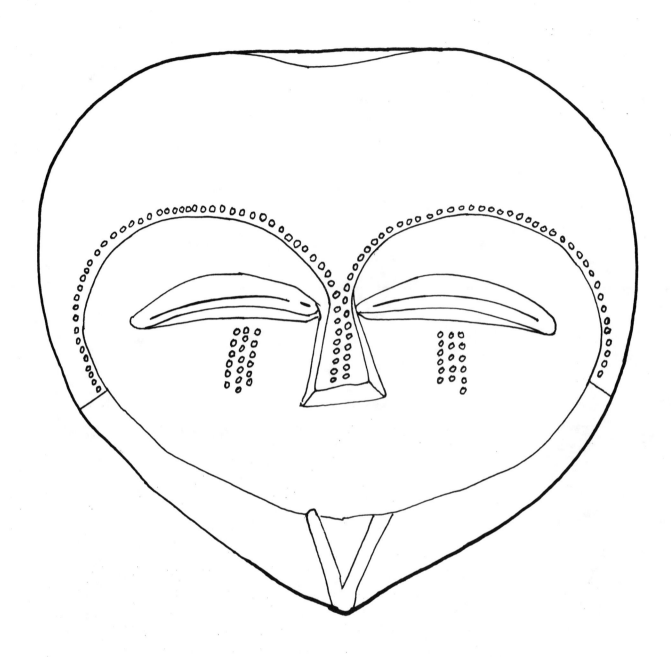

BATEKE

BAKONGO

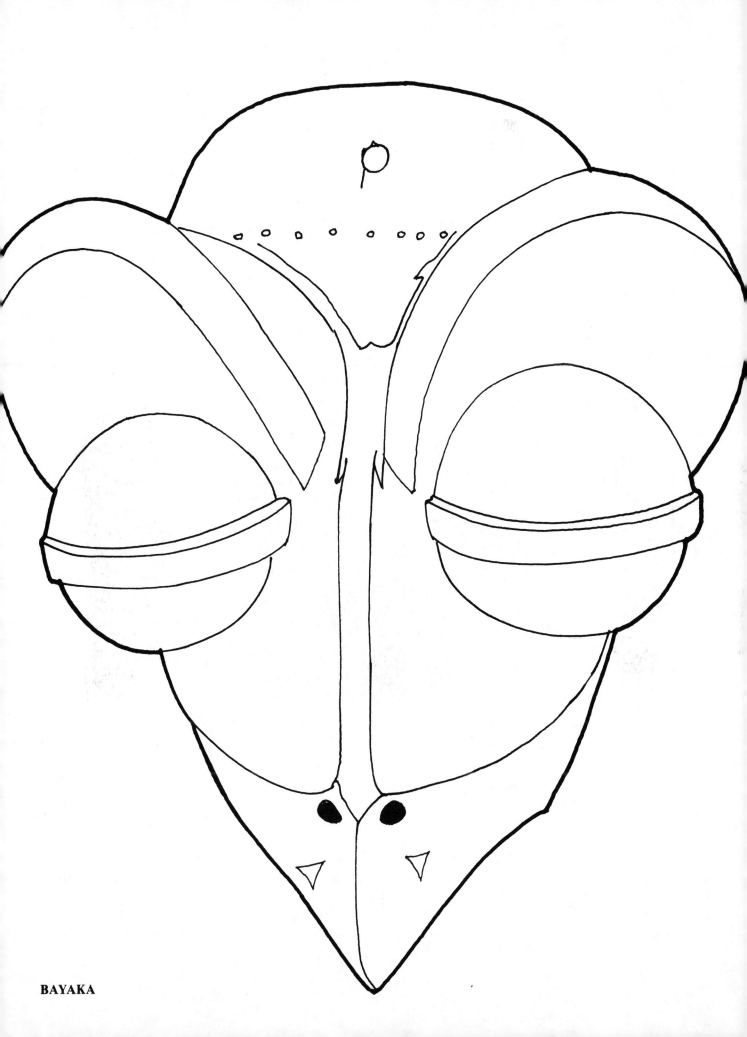

BAYAKA

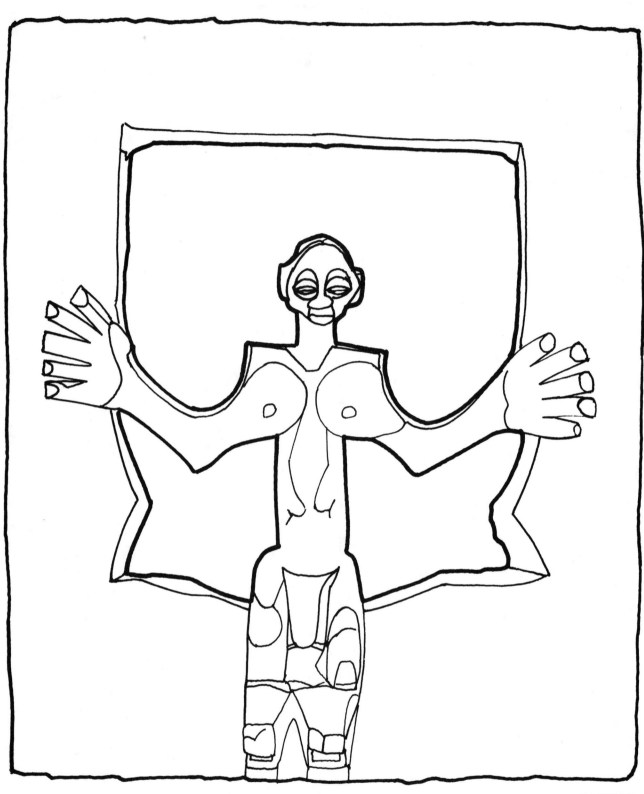

BAHOLO

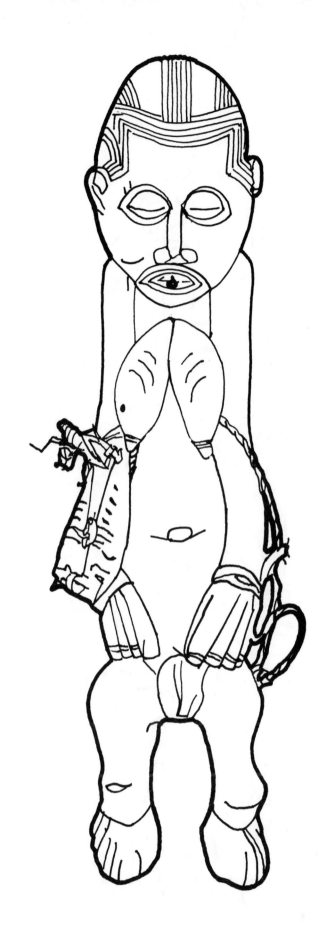

BASUKU

BAPENDE

BUSHONGO

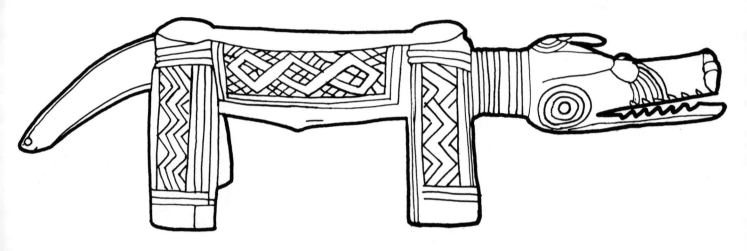

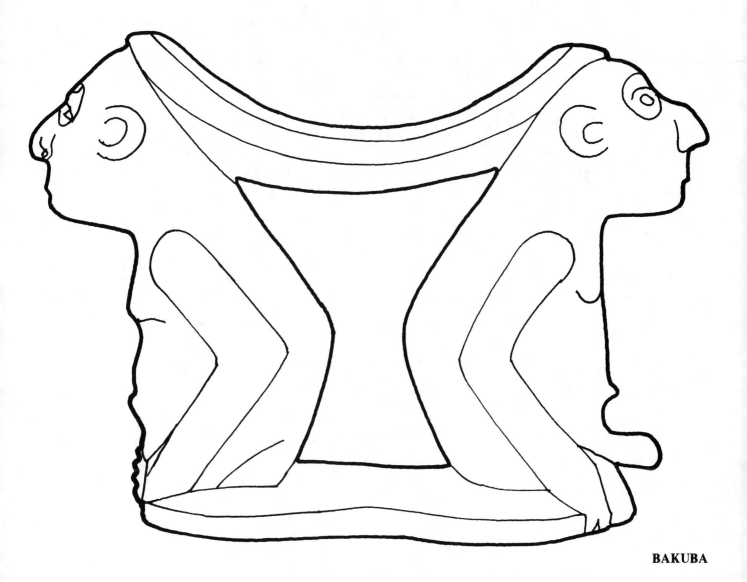

BAKUBA

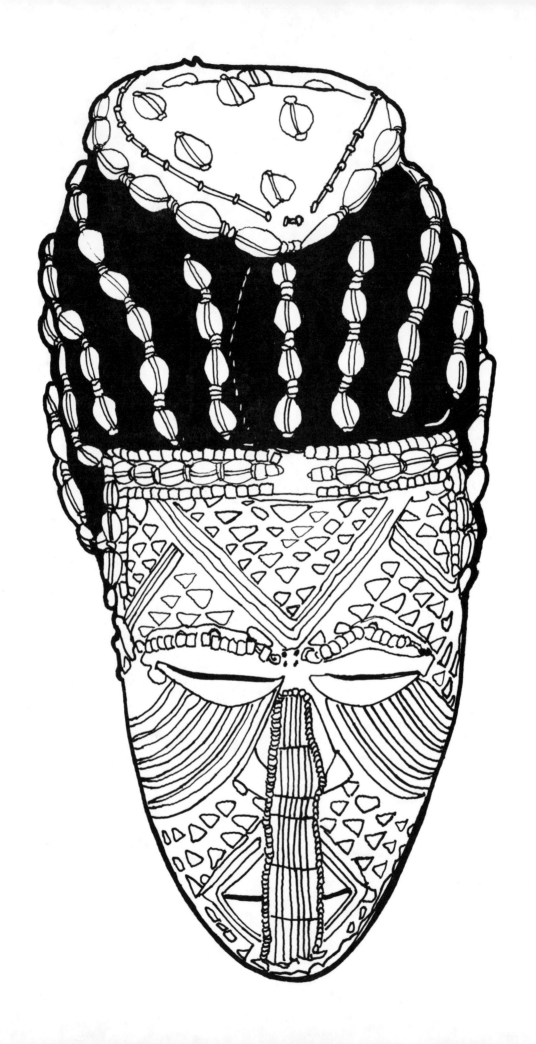

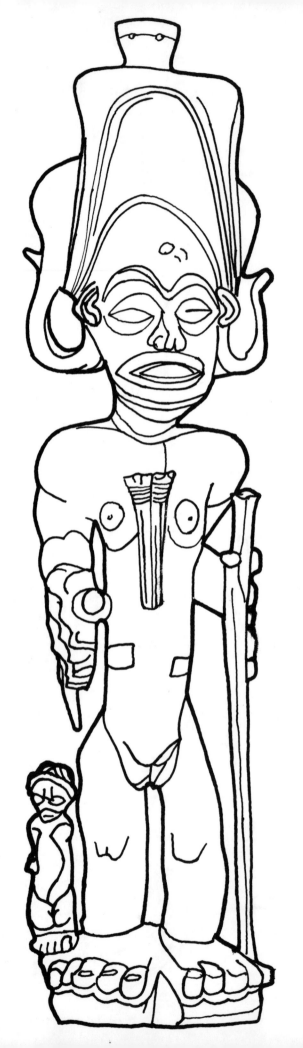

BATCHOKWE

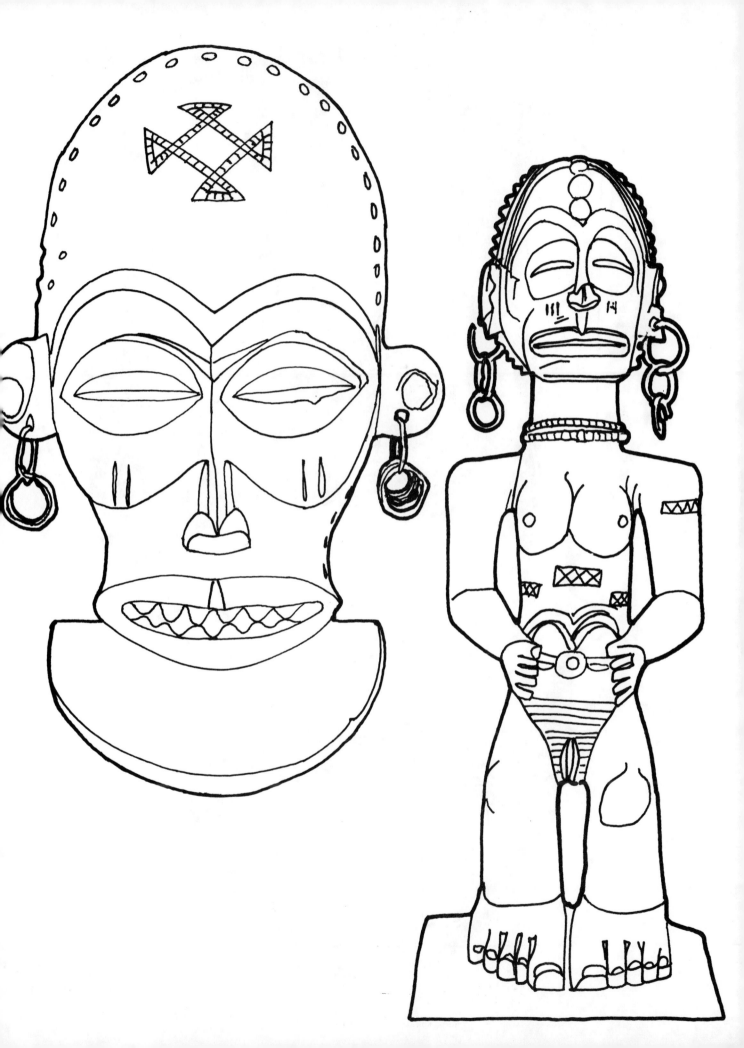

BENA KANIOKA

BASONGE

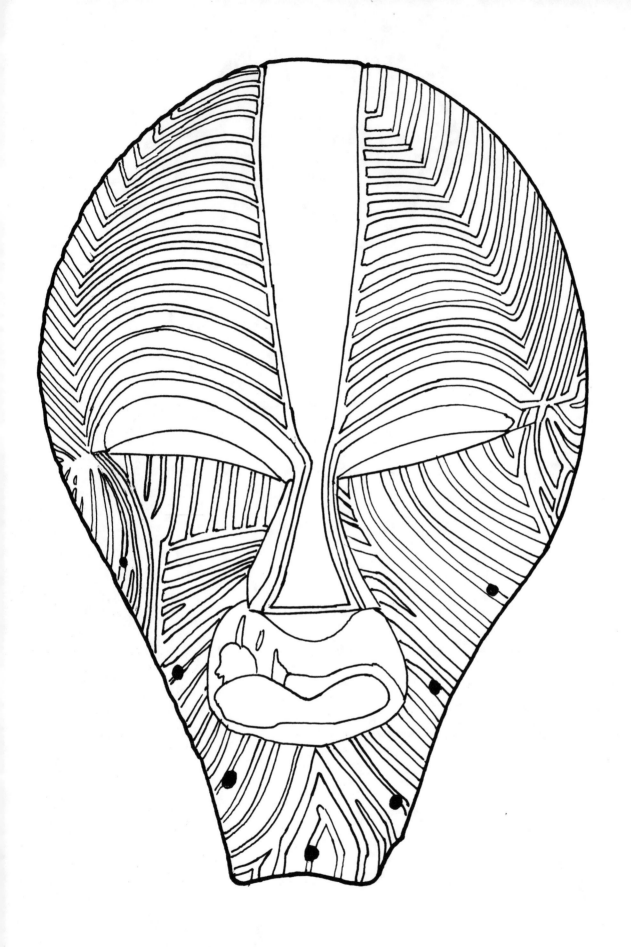

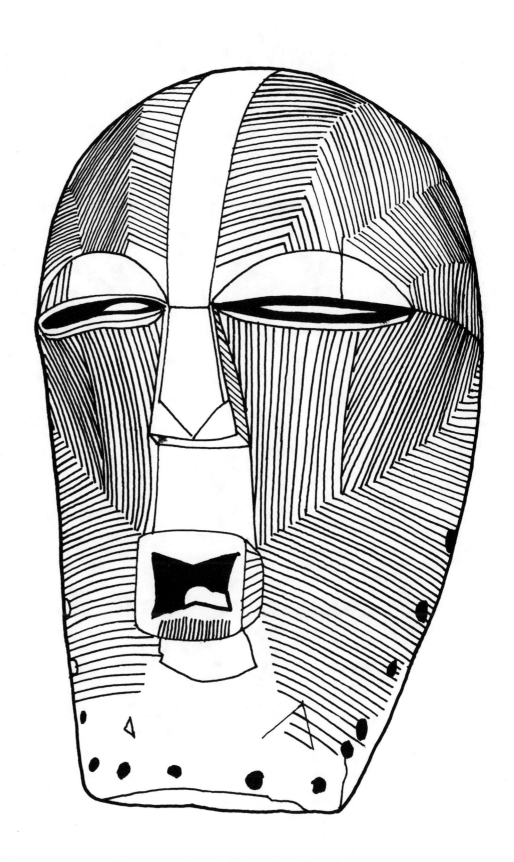

BALUBA

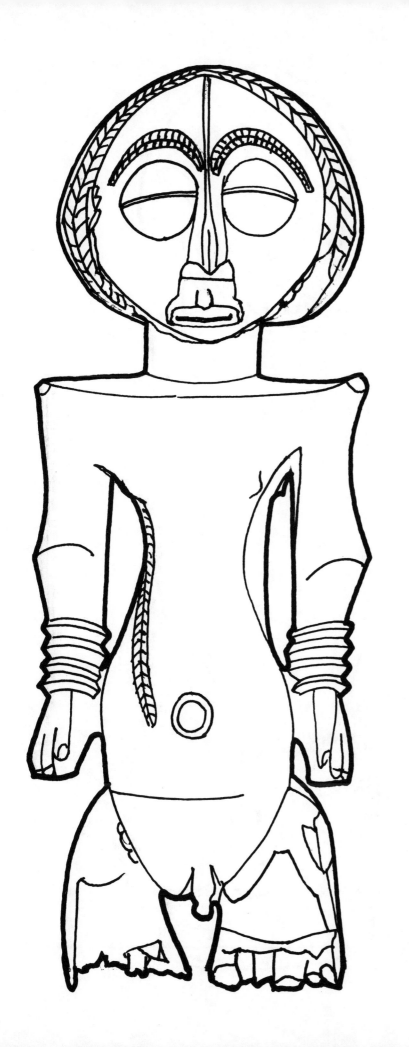

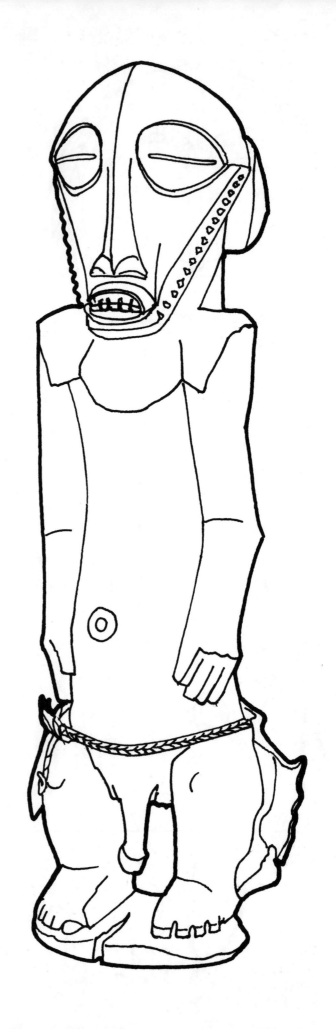

BASIKASINGO

BANGBA

ABABUA

BAMBOLE

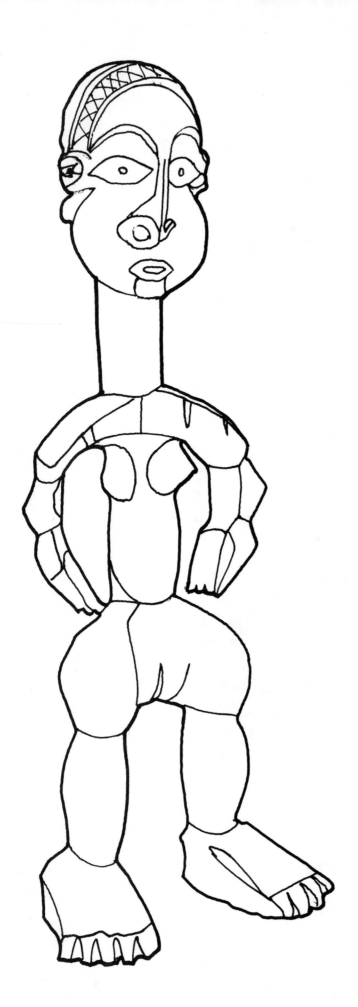

AZENDE

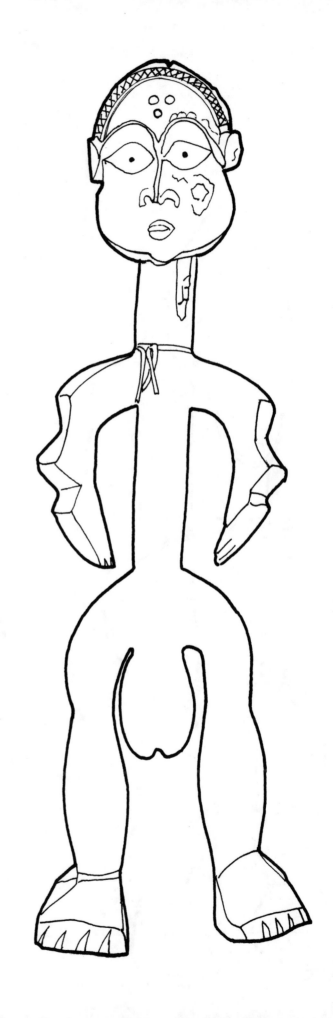

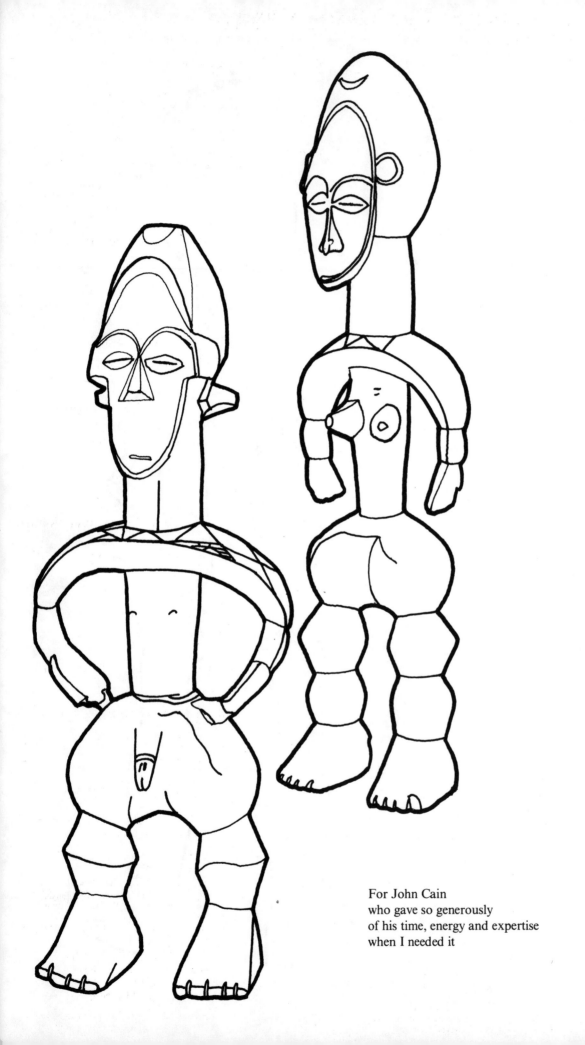

For John Cain
who gave so generously
of his time, energy and expertise
when I needed it